AYRSHIRE & RENFREWSHIRE LOST RAILWAYS

by
Gordon Stansfield

The staff of Mauchline Station, *c.* 1900. From left to right: Muir (first name unknown),
Neil Niven, J. Reid, unknown, W. Harper, W. Breckenbridge, W. Forrester, John Harper.

© Gordon Stansfield 1999
First published in the United Kingdom, 1999,
by Stenlake Publishing, Ochiltree Sawmill, The Lade,
Ochiltree, Ayrshire, KA18 2NX
Telephone / Fax: 01290 423114

ISBN 1 84033 077 5

A class 2P 4-4-0, no. 40667, passing through Milliken Park Station with the 10.13 a.m. service from Glasgow St Enoch to Largs, June 1959.

INTRODUCTION

The first railways came to the counties of Ayr and Renfrew in 1839 and 1840 respectively. Not only did the industries within these areas benefit greatly but a whole new world was opened up to the vast populace of Glasgow and its environs who made their way down to Renfrewshire's pier stations such as Gourock and Greenock Princess Pier or further afield to Ayrshire's coastal resorts of Troon, Ayr and Girvan.

In Renfrewshire the railways were more suburban in nature (although there were through routes from Glasgow to Gourock, Wemyss Bay, Ayr and Stranraer). The Caledonian and Glasgow & South Western were the two operating companies up until 1923 and often competed for traffic to the same destinations. Absurdities in railway construction took place in some instances with lines being built that never saw a passenger train such as the line from Paisley St James to Barrhead.

In Ayrshire competition between the two rival companies was even more intense with each attempting to establish their share of traffic to resorts such as Arran by building different rail routes from Glasgow to Ardrossan. Ayrshire also had more unusual railways such as the Maidens and Dunure Light Railway. Its main purpose was to serve the hotel and golf course at Turnberry and the service provided at one time included a breakfast coach. In later years, once that service had been withdrawn, the line served Butlin's holiday camp at Heads of Ayr which had its own station exclusively for holidaymakers travelling in from as far afield as Newcastle.

After amalgamation of the numerous companies in 1923, Ayrshire and Renfrewshire railways were run by the London, Midland & Scottish Company until nationalisation took place in 1948. Passenger traffic levels in the 1930s continued to be very high, especially on summer Saturdays when the LMS could carry up to 50,000 passengers to the Ayrshire resorts form Glasgow and Paisley.

All this was before the motor cars and bus services changed our travel habits and gone today are many lines to places such as Muirkirk, Catrine, Kilmacolm, Greenock Princess Pier and Renfrew Wharf to name but a few. However, improvements to rail services have occurred. Electrification to Ayr and Largs took place in the late 1980s and brought great benefits to both Renfrewshire and Ayrshire. Closed lines have reopened such as the Paisley Canal route which closed in January 1983 and reopened in July 1990. As for the future, more improvements are planned such as the opening of a rail link from Paisley to Glasgow Airport.

Caldwell Station (later renamed Uplawmoor), July 1955.

PICTURE ACKNOWLEDGEMENTS

The publishers wish to thank the following for contributing photographs to this book: Hugh Brodie for pages 33 and 36; Malcolm Chadwick for the front cover and pages 1, 9, 11, 14-16, 23, 25, 28, 39, 43, 46 and 47; Jean Kennedy for page 4; W.A.C. Smith for pages 2, 3, 6-8, 12, 13, 17-19, 21, 22, 24, 26, 30, 31, 34, 35, 38, 40-42, 45, 48, the inside back cover and the back cover; Neville Stead for pages 5, 10 (photograph by P.B. Booth), 20 (photograph by P.B. Booth), 29, 37 (photograph by A.G. Ellis) and 44.

Annbank – Mauchline (Mauchline Junction)

Passenger service withdrawn	4 January 1943	*Station closed*	*Date*
Distance	6.5 miles	Tarbolton	4 January 1943
Company	Glasgow & South Western		

An extremely rare photograph of Tarbolton Station.

The line between Annbank and Mauchline was the eastern part of the line which connected Ayr with the Glasgow & South Western's route between Glasgow and Carlisle via Kilmarnock at Mauchline. Annbank was a junction where trains travelled via Drongan towards Muirkirk thereby avoiding having to cross the Nithsdale route. There were about four trains daily in each direction between Annbank and Mauchline, all either starting or finishing at Ayr. Despite closure to passenger services in 1943, the line remained open for freight traffic and was put to passenger use in subsequent years for various reasons. In October 1951 it was opened for three weeks to cater for diverted passenger services on the Ayr to Muirkirk line and in the 1950s and '60s it was host to holiday services between Newcastle-upon-Tyne and Butlin's holiday camp at Heads of Ayr on the line from Ayr to Girvan via Turnberry. When the port route from Stranraer to Dumfries closed in June 1965 the through trains for the south which had previously used this route were diverted over the line, having to travel north to Ayr, east to Mauchline and then south to Carlisle. This situation lasted until May 1975 when these services were diverted even further north to Barassie in order that all trains from Stranraer for the south went via Kilmarnock. The line between Annbank and Mauchline was closed to freight in 1983 but reopened in 1988 to cater for new coal traffic.

Passenger service withdrawn	1 April 1868	*Station closed*	*Date*
Distance	5 miles	Newtonhead	1 April 1868
Company	Glasgow & South Western		

A class 2P 4-4-0, no. 40661, at Ardrossan, May 1961.

Ardrossan: Castlehill Junction – Parkhouse Junction

Passenger service withdrawn	18 April 1966
Distance	0.5 miles
Company	Glasgow & South Western

Ardrossan on the Clyde coast was home to two railways – the Caledonian and the Glasgow & South Western. Each company owned a harbour station at Ardrossan, at Montgomerie Pier and Winton Pier respectively. The Glasgow & South Western operated the Largs to Kilwinning line which is still in use today. The section of line from Parkhouse Junction to Castlehill Junction was a spur link from this line on the Largs section in order to join the line from Montgomerie Pier to Ardrossan South Beach Station. This spur was opened in the late 1870s and continued in operation until the closure of the lines to Montgomerie Pier in 1966. There were no stations on this short section.

Ardrossan Montgomerie Pier – Ardrossan (Winton Junction)

Passenger service withdrawn	6 May 1968
Distance	0.5 miles
Company	Caledonian
Stations closed	*Date*
Ardrossan Montgomerie Pier	6 May 1968

This section of line was opened in May 1890 and was constructed in order to give the Caledonian Railway Company access to Ardrossan's Winton Pier Station prior to the construction of the Caledonian's own station at Montgomerie Pier. The line continued in use for passengers until the withdrawal of services to Montgomerie Pier in 1968. Like many other stretches of line during the First World War, services from the pier were suspended from 1 January 1917 until 1 February 1919.

An English Electric Type 1 diesel, no. D8086, passing through Ardrossan North Station on the way to Montgomerie Pier with a 3.00 p.m. special Isle of Arran boat train from Glasgow Central, July 1963.

Ardrossan (Harbour Junction) – Stevenston

Passenger service withdrawn	18 April 1966	*Stations closed*	*Date*
Distance	3.5 miles	Ardrossan North	4 July 1932
Company	Caledonian	Saltcoats North	4 July 1932
		Stevenston Moorpark	4 July 1932

A class 4 2-6-4T, no. 42202, passes the closed station of Saltcoats North with the 8.05 p.m. Belfast boat train from Ardrossan Montgomerie Pier to Glasgow Central, June 1956.

This was the western extent of the Caledonian's line from Glasgow to Ardrossan Montgomerie Pier. The line was originally authorised as part of the Lanarkshire and Ayrshire Railway in 1884 and provided a route shorter by about three miles than the Glasgow to Ardrossan service provided by the Glasgow & South Western. When the line was opened in full in 1888 it was taken over and run by the Caledonian Railway. In competition with the Glasgow & South Western, the stations on the route did not fare well as they were situated on the outskirts of the towns they served rather than at the central locations enjoyed by the Glasgow & South Western's. This was one of the reasons that led to the discontinuation of local passenger services in 1932. In 1947 a short spur line was installed in Stevenston in order that boat trains destined for Montgomerie Pier could leave the Glasgow & South Western line and join the Caledonian line. The last of these ran in September 1965 but the official closure date was 18 April 1966. Station names changed slightly during the years. Ardrossan North was known simply as Ardrossan until 1 October 1906 and thereafter was Ardrossan Town until 2 June 1924. Saltcoats North and Stevenston Moorpark were known simply as Saltcoats and Stevenston until the same date. Although Ardrossan North, Saltcoats North and Stevenston Moorpark were all closed in 1932, when the Caledonian introduced its 'Evening Breathers' services the following year, offering a special return fare of half the single fare, there was such demand by 1934 that these stations had to be reopened specifically to handle the additional traffic.

Barassie (North Junction) – Kilmarnock (Central Junction)

Passenger service withdrawn	3 March 1969	*Stations closed*	*Date*
Distance	8 miles	Drybridge	3 March 1969
Company	Glasgow & South Western	Gatehead	3 March 1969
		Kilmarnock (first)	20 July 1846

A class 4 2-6-4T, no. 42196, at Drybridge with the 5.08 p.m. from Kilmarnock to Ayr and Dalmellington, June 1960.

This line linked the Glasgow & South Western's Ayr to Glasgow line with their Nithsdale route between Glasgow and Carlisle via Kilmarnock. The line began in 1846 when, after a period as a waggonway, it was leased to the Glasgow, Paisley, Kilmarnock and Ayr Railway and regauging was required in order to allow locomotives to operate over the line. In 1899 the Glasgow & South Western took over the route and services running from Ayr to Kilmarnock began. In the 1960s the passenger services consisted of about twelve return journeys between Ayr and Kilmarnock with a Sunday service of four trains. Although the line was closed in 1969, passenger services were reinstated on 5 May 1975 when the Stranraer services to the south were diverted north from the Ayr to Mauchline line in order to serve Kilmarnock.

Gatehead Station, c.1906.

Barassie (South Junction) – Troon (Lochgreen Junction)

Passenger service withdrawn   18 April 1966
Distance   3 miles
Company   Glasgow & South Western

This line was known as the 'Troon Avoiding Line' as it bypassed Troon Station and formed a more direct line on the service from Ayr to Glasgow. Before closure there was just one service which used this line, the 11.00 a.m. Ayr to Glasgow train which only stopped at Prestwick and Paisley Gilmour Street. The goods station at Troon was on this line and continued in use until 1965.

Beith Town – Lugton (North Junction)

Passenger service withdrawn	5 November 1962	*Stations closed*	*Date*
Distance	5 miles	Beith Town	5 November 1962
Company	Glasgow, Barrhead & Kilmarnock Joint Railway	Barrmill	5 November 1962

Beith Town Station, May 1959.

This particular branch was part of the Glasgow, Barrhead and Kilmarnock Joint Line. It was only a branch line for about two miles from Beith to Barrmill. At Barrmill a short line went southwards to join at Giffen with the Ardrossan Line and a branch to Kilbirnie. There was no passenger service over this section to Giffen after 1 May 1903. Services from Beith Town, which was known as Beith until 28 February 1953, went to Glasgow St Enoch. The journey time in 1922 for the nineteen and a half mile trip was about fifty minutes for a semi-fast train. In the few months prior to closure there was one through train to Glasgow St Enoch and vice versa. The remainder of the service amounted to ten short return workings from Beith Town to Lugton where connections were made with trains between Glasgow and Kilmarnock. Right up to the very last day most trains were steam hauled. Freight services along the line lasted until 1964.

Catrine – Mauchline (Brackenhill Junction)

Passenger service withdrawn	3 May 1943	*Station closed*	*Date*
Distance	3.5 miles	Catrine	3 May 1943
Company	Glasgow & South Western		

This postcard of Catrine Station was sent by the lad standing on the engine at the left. He wrote, 'You will notice me standing on the engine with my nippers in my hand. I am working at the station now.'

This short branch line was opened to passengers on 1 September 1903 and provided a service from Catrine to Mauchline where the station was situated on the Glasgow & South Western line from Glasgow St Enoch to Carlisle via Kilmarnock. Apart from connections to stations on this line, passengers could travel westwards to Ayr or south east to Muirkirk. The pattern of services on this Ayrshire branch line allowed for four return journeys Monday to Friday with six on Saturdays. Like other minor passenger lines services were suspended between 1 January 1917 until sometime in 1919 although the actual date is not known. Although passenger services ended in 1943 a railtour special visited the branch in June 1962. Freight services over the line lasted until July 1964.

Cronberry – Auchinleck (Auchinleck Junction)

Passenger service withdrawn	3 July 1950	*Stations closed*	*Date*
Distance	3.75 miles	Lugar	3 July 1950
Company	Glasgow & South Western	Commondyke	3 July 1950

Opened in August 1848, the branch from Cronberry linked the Ayr to Muirkirk line with the Glasgow & South Western's main line from Glasgow to Carlisle via Kilmarnock. Most services originated at Muirkirk where the line continued eastwards toward Lanark and Hamilton. In 1951 passenger services were reinstated for a fortnight to accommodate through trains from Edinburgh to Ayr (these services were withdrawn on 1 October 1951; they had previously run via Drongan). Both Lugar and Commondyke were without freight facilities. In 1976 the line closed completely but there is a prospect that open cast mining will take place in the Douglas Basin near Cronberry in the near future.

A preserved Caledonian Railway 4-2-2, no. 123, on a 'Scottish Rambler' railtour at Skares, April 1962.

Cronberry (Cronberry Junction) – Ayr (Hawkhill Junction)

Passenger service withdrawn	10 September 1951	*Stations closed*	*Date*
Distance	21.25 miles	Skares	10 September 1951
Company	Glasgow & South Western	Ochiltree	10 September 1951
		Drongan	10 September 1951
Stations closed	*Date*	Trabboch	10 September 1951
Cumnock	10 September 1951	Annbank	10 September 1951
Dumfries House	13 June 1949	Auchincruive	10 September 1951

The closed station of Annbank, May 1959, with a 'Land of Burns' railtour standing on the Mauchline line. The line on the right lead to Drongan.

The Ayrshire village of Cronberry was a junction on the line from Muirkirk. One line went from Auchinleck on the Glasgow & South Western main line from Glasgow to Carlisle while the other headed westwards to Annbank where it joined the Mauchline to Ayr line. The portion of the Ayr to Mauchline line as far as Annbank was opened on 1 July 1870 while the section between Cronberry and Annbank was opened on 1 July 1882. The line enjoyed services from as far afield as Edinburgh although these did not begin until after British Railways was established. Muirkirk was the general starting and finishing points of the service and this was where the Caledonian and Glasgow & South Western railways met. After Cumnock Station the line passed under the Glasgow & South Western main line before reaching Belston Junction. It then headed northwards to Annbank and then west to Ayr. Bradshaw's edition of 1922 showed three return journeys between Cronberry and Ayr, all starting or finishing at Muirkirk. There was an additional journey on Saturdays and the running time was just short of an hour. By 1949 there were only two departures from Cronberry – at 7.20 a.m. and 7.13 p.m. Dumfries House and Trabboch stations had no freight facilities but the remaining stations continued to handle freight until 1964, apart from Cumnock's which were withdrawn in July 1959.

Dalmellington – Ayr (Dalrymple Junction)

Passenger service withdrawn	6 April 1964	*Stations closed*	*Date*
Distance	14 miles	Patna (first)	1897
Company	Glasgow & South Western	Patna	6 April 1964
		Holehouse Junction	3 April 1950
Stations closed	*Date*	Hollybush	6 April 1964
Dalmellington	6 April 1964	Dalrymple Junction	1 December 1859
Waterside	6 April 1964		

Dalmellington Station.

This branch line was built mainly for the benefit of the Dalmellington Iron Company who had a large number of works in this area, especially at Waterside. Opened to passengers in 1856, the line became part of the Glasgow & South Western in August 1858. The passenger service was somewhat limited as the bulk of traffic was coal from the various collieries in the area. Holehouse Junction Station was unusual as it was an exchange platform only, linking the Dalmellington branch with the village of Rankinston. Further east from Rankinston was Belston Junction which was on the line from Cronberry to Annbank. The service to Rankinston was withdrawn in 1950. In 1918 the Government considered improving rural transport in Scotland and the scheme suggested constructing a light railway to link Dalmellington with Parton on the Dumfries to Stranraer line, but no progress was made. Freight services were withdrawn three months after passengers services but after closure the line lasted until 1978 due to the use of coal trains from Minnivey Colliery at Dalmellington.

The Station, Waterside *c*.1930

Dalry (Brownhill Junction) – Elderslie (Cart Junction)

Passenger service withdrawn	27 June 1966	*Stations closed*	*Date*
Distance	13.5 miles	Kilbirnie	27 June 1966
Company	Glasgow & South Western	Lochwinnoch	27 June 1966
		Kilbarchan	27 June 1966
		Johnstone North	7 March 1955

Lochwinnoch Station, *c.* **1918.**

This line, which travelled between Ayrshire and Renfrewshire, left the existing Ayr to Glasgow route at Brownhill Junction near Dalry before rejoining the same line at Elderslie. Elderslie Station was at the junction and it was also the starting point for the lines to Kilmacolm and Greenock Princess Pier in the west and the Paisley Canal line in the east. The line, opened to passengers on 1 June 1905, was built as relief to the existing route between Paisley and Kilwinning as the traffic over this section was very dense. Kilbirnie had two stations, the other being the branch line terminus of a Caledonian line from Giffen which provided services to Glasgow Central, while the Glasgow and South Western's station ran trains to Glasgow St Enoch. The Caledonian branch lost its passenger service in 1930. In the few years prior to closure the line had about twelve return passenger journeys with trains coming from Glasgow St Enoch to Kilmarnock, Ayr, Ardrossan or Largs. Freight services along the line were withdrawn before the passenger services apart from those at Lochwinnoch which lasted until 1969. Today part of the route forms a cycleway through Ayrshire and Renfrewshire.

A Black Five 4-6-0, no. 44992, at Kilbirnie Station with the 6.00 p.m. from Glasgow St Enoch to Kilmarnock via Dalry, July 1963.

Dalry (Dalry Junction) – Kilmarnock (Central Junction)

Passenger service withdrawn	23 October 1973	*Stations closed*	*Date*
Distance	11 miles	Montgreenan	7 March 1955
Company	Glasgow & South Western	Cunninghamhead	1 January 1951
		Crosshouse	18 April 1966

The closed station of Cunninghamhead, February 1963.

This north Ayrshire cross country route linked the Glasgow & South Western's Glasgow to Ayr line with their Glasgow to Carlisle via Kilmarnock line. The pattern of services along the line allowed for Glasgow to Kilmarnock trains to travel via Paisley and Lochwinnoch or Beith. There were very few passenger trains which went over this line and the last local service was withdrawn in April 1966. However, certain through trains did use the line until closure in October 1973. Freight services were withdrawn from Montgreenan in October 1955, from Cunninghamhead in February 1960 and from Crosshouse in July 1964. Crosshouse was a junction station where trains from Kilmarnock could proceed to the Glasgow & South Western line near Irvine. The service along this line was withdrawn in April 1964.

A Park Royal railbus at Crosshouse forming the 9.51 a.m. service from Ardrossan North to Kilmarnock, April 1962.

Darvel – Hurlford (Galston Branch Junction)

Passenger service withdrawn	6 April 1964	*Stations closed*	*Date*
Distance	7.25 miles	Darvel	6 April 1964
Company	Glasgow & South Western	Newmilns	6 April 1964
		Galston	6 April 1964
		Barleith	6 April 1964

A class 2P 4-4-0, no. 40688, with the 7.05 p.m. service to Kilmarnock at Darvel Station, May 1959.

Darvel was the Glasgow & South Western's second last station on its section of the route from Kilmarnock to Strathaven which joined the Caledonian Railway Company's line at the County Boundary Junction between Loudonhill Station on the Glasgow and South Western line and Drumclog Station on the Caledonian's route from Lanark. County Boundary Junction was on the geographical border between Lanarkshire and Ayrshire. The line opened on 1 June 1896 but the Caledonian's service did not begin until 1 May 1905. There were no through trains between Kilmarnock and Strathaven but the service between Darvel and Strathaven was jointly provided by the two companies who had an agreement that they would take turns to work the line every six months. The services operating from Darvel extended further than Kilmarnock with many trains continuing to Glasgow St Enoch. In the early 1960s the line had a mixture of rolling stock ranging from railbuses and diesel multiple units to steam trains. Indeed on the last day of passenger services the 5.12 p.m. from Darvel consisted of one coach pulled by BR locomotive no. 80077. Barleith, known as Barleith Halt until January 1954, was opened by the London, Midland & Scottish Railway and had no freight facilities.

A class 2P 4-4-0, no. 40570, at Galston Station with the 6.06 p.m. service from Kilmarnock, July 1958.

A standard tank, no. 80077, comes into Barleith Station with the 4.00 p.m. from Ardrossan North to Darvel on 4 April, 1964 – the last day of service.

Fairlie Pier – Fairlie High (Fairlie Pier Junction)

Passenger service withdrawn   1 October 1971   *Station closed*   *Date*
Distance   0.5 miles   Fairlie Pier   1 October 1971
Company   Glasgow & South Western

Fairlie Pier from Craig Hill

This short branch ran from Fairlie Pier to the village's High Station which stood on the line between Ardrossan and Largs. The pier was run by the Glasgow & South Western and from it shipping services ran to various Clyde coast destinations such as Millport and the Isle of Bute. The line opened in July 1882 and many trains ran non-stop from Glasgow St Enoch to Fairlie Pier. In the winter months the Arran service to Brodick left from Fairlie Pier rather than Ardrossan Pier and right up to the 1960s the pier was required along with several others to handle the Clyde coast traffic. However, with changes to travel patterns and the introduction of Ro/Ro ships to many of the routes in the early 1970s, it was decided that Fairlie Pier could be dispensed with and services to the Isle of Cumbrae were run from a new slipway at Largs with a bus connection into Millport. The last steamer service ran from Fairlie Pier in March 1972 although the last passenger train had run the previous year. The official closure date for passenger services was 31 January 1972 but in reality they ended on 1 October 1971.

Giffen (Giffen Junction) – Barrmill (Barrmill Junction)

Passenger service withdrawn	1 May 1903	*Company*	Caledonian
Distance	0.5 miles		

This half mile line was the last stage before the Caledonian line from Ardrossan joined the Glasgow, Barrhead and Kilmarnock joint line at Barrmill Junction. The Caledonian resented having to pay for the use of this line and in 1903 opened its own line from Giffen. This ran parallel to the Glasgow, Barrhead and Kilmarnock's line for a while before reaching Lugton and Neilston. This allowed the Caledonian to run through trains on its own metals between Ardrossan and Glasgow, thereby making the link between the two junctions surplus to requirements.

A class 2P 4-4-0, no. 40617, at Barrmill Station with the 7.25 p.m. Beith Town to Lugton service, September 1955.

Girvan Old – Girvan Junction

Passenger service withdrawn	1 April 1893
Distance	0.5 miles
Company	Glasgow & South Western
Station closed	*Date*
Girvan Old	1 April 1893

The station known as Girvan Old was Girvan's first and consisted of a single platform. This was the terminus of the Maybole & Girvan Railway which was opened to passengers in May 1860 and worked by the Glasgow & South Western. When the line to Stranraer from Girvan was opened in 1877 trains still called at both Girvan Old and Girvan New Station. This involved trains from Stranraer backing into the branch line from Girvan Junction while trains coming from the Ayr direction had to back out. The line between Girvan and Stranraer was owned initially by the Girvan & Portpatrick Joint Railway Company and then, from 1877, the Ayrshire & Wigtownshire. When the Glasgow & South Western acquired the line it decided to close Girvan Old in favour of the New which remains in use today.

Girvan (Girvan North Junction) – Turnberry

Passenger service withdrawn	2 March 1942	*Company*	Glasgow & South Western
Distance	5 miles		

Turnberry Hotel was established by the Glasgow & South Western in order to cater for a well-to-do tourist market and they were transported in by means of a light railway which left the Ayr to Stranraer line at Alloway Junction and rejoined it at Girvan. This line, known as the Maidens line as it also served the small village of the same name, was opened throughout in May 1906. When it came to closure the line was truncated into sections. The first closure was the section between Ayr and Turnberry in December 1930 but this was short-lived as the stretch reopened between July 1932 and March 1933 for two through trains that ran daily between Kilmarnock and Turnberry. The intermediate stations which had closed in 1930 did not reopen.

Railway Station, Alloway

Heads of Ayr – Ayr (Alloway Junction)

Passenger service withdrawn	7 September 1968	*Stations closed*	*Date*
Distance	3.25 miles	Heads of Ayr	7 September 1968
Company	Glasgow & South Western	Alloway	1 December 1930

This line formed part of the northerly section of the light railway. Heads of Ayr Station was the second station to be built at this location and was opened by the London Midland & Scottish Railway to serve a naval base which was established during the Second World War. After the base was closed, the station was acquired by Butlin's and used by holidaymakers travelling to their camp from Glasgow and further afield. With the increased use of coaches to serve the holiday camp passengers, passenger services were withdrawn after the end of the summer season in 1968.

Holehouse (Holehouse Junction) – Ochiltree (Belston Junction)

Passenger service withdrawn	3 April 1950
Distance	4 miles
Company	Glasgow & South Western

Stations closed	*Date*
Rankinston	3 April 1950
Cairntable Halt	3 April 1950

This Ayrshire line left the Ayr to Dalmellington branch line at Holehouse before striking eastwards to join the line from Annbank to Cronberry at Belston Junction. Opened in 1872, the line provided an important link between the two branches especially for the large amount of coal traffic in the area. The passenger service along the line was very fragmented as Holehouse Junction was an exchange platform only where passengers could change for trains to Ayr or Dalmellington.

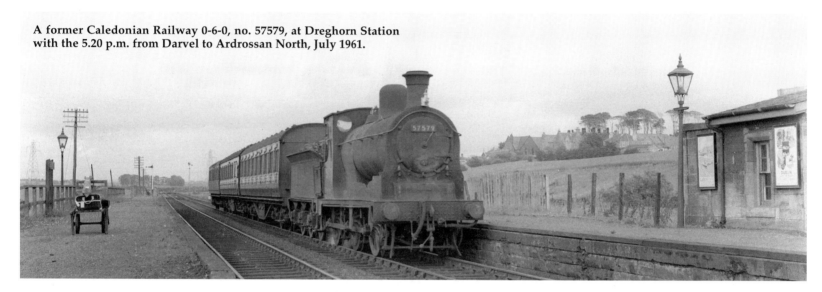

A former Caledonian Railway 0-6-0, no. 57579, at Dreghorn Station with the 5.20 p.m. from Darvel to Ardrossan North, July 1961.

Irvine (Irvine Junction) – Crosshouse (Crosshouse Junction)

Passenger service withdrawn	6 April 1964
Distance	5.5 miles
Company	Glasgow & South Western

Stations closed	*Date*
Dreghorn	6 April 1964
Springside	6 April 1964

This line left the Glasgow to Ayr line at Irvine before heading eastwards to Kilmarnock and joining the line from Dalry to Kilmarnock (closed to passengers 1973) at Crosshouse. Opened in May 1848, the line had two intermediate stations at Dreghorn and Springside although the latter had no freight facilities. In the 1920s the pattern of service allowed for trains to run from Kilmarnock to Ardrossan along this route, a situation which continued right up until closure. The last timetable for the route had ten return journeys which included connections with the Clyde coast steamer services to Arran and Millport on the Isle of Cumbrae. The line closed completely in October 1965.

Irvine (Byrehill Junction) – Stevenston (Dubbs Junction)

Passenger service withdrawn	6 April 1964
Distance	2 miles
Company	Glasgow & South Western

This loop allowed trains coming from Ayr to Glasgow to join the line from Kilwinning to Largs without the need to reverse at Kilwinning. The main service which used the line were trains from Kilmarnock to Ardrossan and although this service was withdrawn in April 1964, the line remained open for passenger traffic until June 1977.

Irvine (Bank Street) – Kilwinning (Kilwinning Junction)

Passenger service withdrawn	28 July 1930	*Stations closed*	*Date*
Distance	3.25 miles	Irvine Bank Street	28 July 1930
Company	Caledonian	Bogside Moor Halt	28 July 1930

This branch line ran from Kilwinning East Station on the Caledonian's line from Ardrossan to Glasgow via Giffen (which lost its local passenger service in July 1932) and encroached into what was prominent Glasgow & South Western territory. The service between Kilwinning and Irvine was operated by one locomotive and one coach and became known by the locals as the 'Riviera Express'. When the line opened to passengers in 1890 there were no intermediate stations but an intermediate halt was opened at Bogside in 1901 where trains only called upon request. In June 1924, in order to avoid confusion with the stations on the ex-Glasgow & South Western route to Ayr, both Irvine and Bogside had their names changed to Irvine Bank Street and Bogside Moor Halt, the latter became known simply as Bogside Halt. It had no freight facilities and the whole line had been closed for reasons of wartime economy from January 1917 until February 1919. The branch closed completely in 1939.

This postcard was captioned 'Kilbirnie, 1936' and is believed to show the closed station of Kilbirnie South.

Kilbirnie South – Giffen (Giffen South Junction)

Passenger service withdrawn	1 December 1930		*Stations closed*	*Date*
Distance	4.5 miles		Kilbirnie South	1 December 1930
Company	Caledonian		Glengarnock High	1 December 1930
			Brackenhills	1 December 1930

Kilbirnie was in the heart of the Glasgow & South Western's territory. The Caledonian was keen to make inroads into this lucrative area and with the opening of their line to Ardrossan, the opportunity arose to construct a short branch from Giffen. This opened to passengers on 2 December 1889 and at first had just two stations; Brackenhills became the third on 1 September 1906. When the London Midland & Scottish took control of the line following the Railway Act, in order to avoid confusion with the ex-Glasgow & South Western stations of the same name, Kilwinning was changed to Kilwinning South and Glengarnock was changed to Glengarnock High as of 2 June 1924. The line was expensive to construct and traffic was light; the service provided was a shuttle service to Giffen with the four and a half mile trip taking about a quarter of an hour. There were about nine return journeys on weekdays with two extra on Saturdays. Freight services were withdrawn on the same date as the passenger services apart from at Glengarnock High which continued to accept freight services until 1945.

Platform View of Railway Station, Cronberry.

BB51

Muirkirk – Cronberry

Passenger service withdrawn	1 October 1951	*Stations closed*	*Date*
Distance	6.5 miles	Muirkirk (first)	1896
Company	Glasgow & South Western	Cronberry	10 September 1951

Muirkirk Station, May 1959.

The line from Muirkirk to Cronberry formed part of the route which ran from Lanark to Ayr. Owned by two railway companies – the Caledonian (from Lanark to Muirkirk) and the Glasgow & South Western (from Muirkirk to Ayr), Muirkirk was the usual point where passengers changed trains. Cronberry was a junction where trains could go to Auchinleck on the Glasgow and South Western main line from Glasgow to Carlisle via Dumfries, or to Annbank where it could join the Mauchline to Ayr line. Local services to Ayr from Muirkirk ran via Drongan and were withdrawn in 1951.

Muirkirk – Lanark (Smyllum West Junction) *

Passenger service withdrawn	5 October 1964	*Stations closed*	*Date*
Distance	18.75 miles	Muirkirk	5 October 1964
Company	Glasgow & South Western/Caledonian	Glenbuck	4 August 1952

A class of locomotive rarely seen in Scotland, this is a Fowler 2-6-2T, no. 40049, at Glenbuck with the 4.56 p.m. from Muirkirk to Lanark, May 1959.

The line from Muirkirk to Lanark was the easterly section of the route which ran from Ayr and allowed through trains to run between Ayrshire and Edinburgh. The section of route in Ayrshire was opened by the Glasgow & South Western, including Muirkirk station, while the rest of the line was owned by the Caledonian. The first through trains to Muirkirk began in June 1874. Just past Muirkirk was a junction which formed a route to Coalburn. Known as the Spyreslack branch line, it was built by the Caledonian but they never brought it into use as they feared that the Glasgow & South Western would seek running powers over it. With the demise in coal and mineral traffic in the early part of the twentieth century, Muirkirk's population decreased and so did its passenger traffic but nonetheless a passenger service was maintained right up until 1964. The last passenger timetable for the line gave five return trips between Lanark and Muirkirk on weekdays.

* Once into Lanarkshire the line passed through the stations of Inches, Douglas West, Happendon, Ponfeigh and Sandilands before reaching Lanark. Details of these stations appear in *Lanarkshire's Lost Railways*.

Stevenston – Uplawmoor (East Junction)

Passenger service withdrawn	16 June 1947	*Stations closed*	*Date*
Distance	13 miles	Kilwinning East	4 July 1932
Company	Caledonian	Auchenmade	4 July 1932
		Giffen	4 July 1932
		Lugton (High)	4 July 1932

The partly demolished Kilwinning East Station, June 1955

This line was the eastern extremity of the Caledonian's attempt to encroach upon prominent Glasgow & South Western territory by constructing a line to Ardrossan. Most of the stations on the line duplicated those of the Glasgow & South Western, such as Kilwinning East which was known as Kilwinning, and Lugton High which was known as Lugton until June 1924. The local service from Glasgow to Ardrossan by this route was withdrawn in 1932 but some boat trains continued to use the line until June 1947 when a short spur was installed at Stevenston which allowed these trains to run on the Glasgow & South Western metals to Stevenston and then the Caledonian's to Ardrossan. Freight services to Auchenmade and Giffen lasted until 1953.

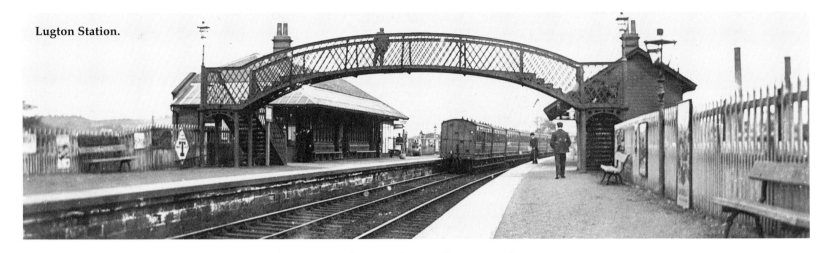

Lugton Station.

Strathaven Central – Darvel

Passenger service withdrawn	11 September 1939	*Station closed*	*Date*
Distance	10.5 miles	Loudonhill	11 September 1939
Company	Caledonian/Glasgow & South Western		

Opened on 1 May 1905 this line was known as the Strathaven and Darvel railway. The line crossed the boundary of the Caledonian and Glasgow & South Western at County Boundary Junction but in fact there was no junction at this location. Great plans had been made for this line as it was envisaged as providing a through route between Lanarkshire and Ayrshire. It all came to nothing as there was very little traffic along the route. Local services were poorly patronised simply because there was no population in the area. The three stations on the route were all closed from September until November 1909 and again from January 1917 until December 1922. Services ran to Darvel from Kilmarnock until April 1964. Although the last passenger services ran on 10 September 1939 the actual official closing date was two weeks later. Freight services were withdrawn at the same time as the passenger service and the line lifted shortly afterwards.

Troon Harbour – Barassie (Middle Junction)

Passenger service withdrawn	October 1850
Distance	1.5 miles
Company	Glasgow, Paisley, Kilmarnock & Ayr Railway
Station closed	*Date*
Troon Harbour	October 1850

Opened in 1812, this line formed part of the original Kilmarnock to Troon waggonway on which the waggons were horse-drawn. In July 1846 the waggonway was leased to the Glasgow, Paisley, Kilmarnock and Ayr Railway who regauged the line for locomotives. However, it was decided that a service to Troon Harbour for passengers was not required so the line was cut back to Barassie in 1850.

Turnberry – Heads of Ayr

Passenger service withdrawn	1 June 1933	Stations closed	Date
Distance	10.5 miles	Maidens	1 December 1930
Company	Glasgow & South Western	Glenside	1 December 1930
		Balchriston level Crossing Halt	1 December 1930
		Knoweside	1 December 1930
		Dunure	1 December 1930
		Heads of Ayr (first)	1 December 1930

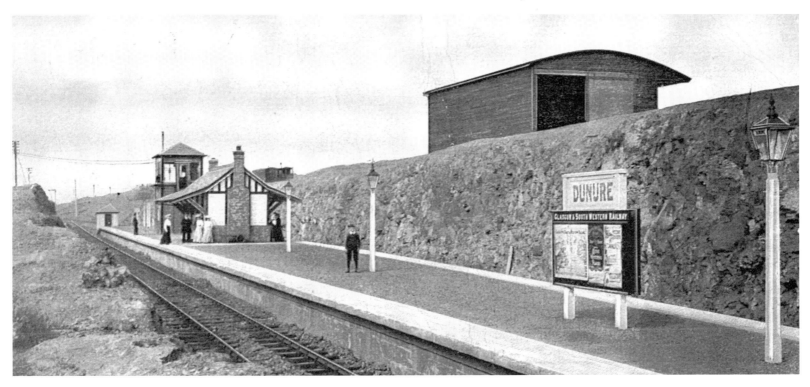

In the early 1920s there were eight return journeys along the Maidens line including a breakfast car on the early service train from Turnberry which ran through to Glasgow St Enoch. The return journey featured a tea car which left St Enoch at 5.10 p.m., arriving at Turnberry at 6.40 p.m. Local passenger services were withdrawn in December 1930 but through services were reinstated in July 1932 for two through trains daily between Kilmarnock and Turnberry. This lasted until 1933 when the passenger service was finally withdrawn. Freight services lasted until 1955.

Barrhead: North Junction – South Junction

Passenger service withdrawn	1 October 1907	*Company*	Glasgow & South Western
Distance	0.5 miles		

This short line between the two junctions at Barrhead was part of the ill-fated suburban services which operated in the Paisley and Barrhead area. On 1 October 1902 a circular service began between Glasgow St Enoch, Potterhill, Barrhead Central, Pollockshaws and Glasgow St Enoch. Known as the Barrhead circular service it only lasted five years until 1 October 1907. The services which used this line were not very profitable but behind the construction of the line and the provision of services was a conflict between the two main railway operators in the area – the Glasgow & South Western and the Caledonian. This situation became known as the Battle of the Braes. Indeed the Caledonian built a line on the western outskirts of Paisley towards Barrhead, building stations at Ferguslie, Stanley and Glenfield which were never put into passenger use.

Barrhead Central – Barrhead (North Junction)

Passenger service withdrawn	1 January 1917	*Station closed*	*Date*
Distance	0.75 miles	Barrhead Central	1 January 1917
Company	Glasgow & South Western		

A Black Five, no. 44996, at Paisley West Station with the 5.33 p.m. from Glasgow St Enoch to Kilmarnock via Dalry, August 1963.

This station was opened by the Glasgow & South Western upon the introduction of its Glasgow St Enoch – Potterhill – Barrhead Central – Pollockshaws – Glasgow St Enoch circular service. Barrhead Central had a very short life span as far as railway stations go. The circular service was withdrawn on 1 October 1907 but a service remained from Potterhill to Barrhead Central until 1 February 1913. The remains of the circular service from Glasgow St Enoch – Barrhead Central via Pollockshaws continued until the end of 1916. Within a few years Barrhead and Paisley had several suburban services which were never very viable due to the expansion of electric tramcar services which in the end forced the railway to curtail its operation in this area.

Elderslie (Canal Junction) – Glasgow (Shields Junction)

Passenger service withdrawn	10 January 1983
Distance	8.5 miles
Company	Glasgow & South Western

Stations closed	*Date*
Paisley West	14 February 1966
Paisley Canal	10 January 1983
Hawkhead	14 February 1966
Crookston	10 January 1983
Mosspark West	10 January 1983
Corkerhill	10 January 1983

Opened in July 1885 this line was known as the Paisley Canal Line. Starting at Elderslie Station on the Glasgow & South Western's main line from Glasgow St Enoch to Ayr, the line wound its way through the southern suburbs of Paisley and Glasgow, rejoining the same line at Shields Junction. The Glasgow & South Western envisaged that it would form part of a circular service linking Glasgow, Barrhead and Paisley but the services did not last long due to the rapid development of tram routes in the area. They were also in competition with the Caledonian for the traffic in the area and the Caledonian had its own proposals for new lines. However, all these came to nothing in the end and by the mid-1920s the Paisley Canal Line had lost its links with other passenger lines along its route. All the stations were opened by the Glasgow & South Western apart from the Glasgow stations on the line which were operated by the London, Midland & Scottish Railway. In 1991 Strathclyde Passenger Transport Executive partly reopened the line by providing a service from Glasgow Central to Paisley Canal with stations reopened or replaced at Paisley Canal, Hawkhead, Crookston, Mosspark West and Corkerhill.

Greenock Princess Pier – Kilmacolm

Passenger service withdrawn	14 February 1966
Distance	8 miles
Company	Glasgow & South Western

Stations closed	*Date*
Greenock Princes Pier (first)	25 May 1894
Greenock Princess Pier	2 February 1959
Greenock Lynedoch	2 February 1959

This line formed the western extremity of the Glasgow & South Western route from Glasgow St Enoch to Greenock via Paisley Canal and Kilmacolm. Greenock had been the stronghold of the Caledonian but the Glasgow & South Western made an inroad by building an impressive station at Princess Pier which allowed it to gain some of the Clyde coast steamer traffic. The Caledonian's station was badly situated as passengers were required to go to Customs House Quay to catch its steamer services. Steamer services continued to run to the Clyde coast resorts until 1952 when these services were abandoned. However, local passenger train services continued until 1959. In the late 1950s and early 1960s Princess Pier dealt with passenger liners from across the Atlantic and upon arrival passengers were conveyed in special ocean liner boat trains to Glasgow. After the withdrawal of passenger services the pier became a container depot. The service to Kilmacolm lasted until January 1983.

A Standard tank, no. 80024, awaits departure at Greenock Princess Pier with the 8.45 p.m. for Glasgow St Enoch, July 1954.

Johnstone North – Elderslie (Cart Junction)

Passenger service withdrawn	1 June 1905
Distance	1.25 miles
Company	Glasgow & South Western

Station closed	*Date*
Johnstone North (first)	1 June 1905

Opened on 1 August 1886, this line was a short branch which remained in use until a new loop line was opened in tandem with the new Johnstone North Station in 1905. This loop line was designed to help alleviate the high traffic volumes over the Glasgow to Ayr route between Paisley and Dalry and continued south to join that line at Todhills Junction near Dalry.

Kilmacolm – Elderslie (Cart Junction)

Passenger service withdrawn	10 January 1983
Distance	7.75 miles
Company	Glasgow & South Western

Stations closed	*Date*
Kilmacolm	10 January 1983
Bridge of Weir (first)	18 May 1868
Bridge of Weir	10 January 1983
Houston and Crosslee	10 January 1983

Kilmacolm Station.

This was the central section of the Glasgow & South Western line which ran from Glasgow St Enoch to Greenock Princess Pier. The westerly section from Princess Pier to Kilmacolm closed to local passenger services in 1959 but was used by ocean liner trains in the early 1960s. Trains from Kilmacolm ran to Glasgow St Enoch via the Paisley Canal line and although the line closed to passengers in 1983 the easterly section from Paisley Canal to Glasgow reopened in April 1991. The first station at Bridge of Weir closed in May 1868 when the line was extended to Princess Pier in Greenock. Houston and Crosslee station went through several name changes: it was known as Windyhill until May 1871, Crosslee until January 1874, Houston until January 1875, Houston (Crosslee) until 1926 and Houston again until May 1973. In the middle 1960s there were about fifteen return journeys to and from Kilmacolm. Freight services were withdrawn from Kilmacolm in May 1965 and in October 1965 from Bridge of Weir and Houston and Crosslee.

Paisley St James – Barrhead (Lyoncross Junction)

Company   Caledonian

Glenfield station was on the line which left the Glasgow to Greenock route at Paisley St James Station. Heading south, the line passed near Paisley's Gleniffer Braes before reaching Barrhead. Built at the turn of the century, the line never provided a passenger service although stations with all facilities were built at Ferguslie, Stanely, Glenfield, Barrhead New and Barrhead South. In addition the line was signalled throughout with signal boxes that were never really required. The Caledonian Railway company who were responsible for the line had hoped to provide a circular suburban passenger service from Glasgow – Barrhead – Paisley – Glasgow but the competition from the trams rendered the route obsolete before services could begin. Although the line never saw regular passenger services occasional Sunday school outings in the 1950s used the stations as a starting point for trips to the Clyde coast resorts. The northern section of the route remained in use into the 1960s to the Rootes car factory at Linwood which also made the bodies for Glasgow's 'Blue Trains' which entered service in 1960.

Glenfield Station, September 1951.

Potterhill – Barrhead (South Junction)

Passenger service withdrawn	1 June 1913	*Company*	Glasgow & South Western
Distance	1.75 miles		

This line formed the southern section of the ill-fated suburban services which were operated by the Glasgow & South Western. The intention was to provide a suburban railway circular service linking Glasgow St Enoch, Nitshill, Barrhead and Paisley with the latter section using the Paisley Canal line which is still in use today. October 1902 saw the start of these services but by 1913 it was decided that the section south of Potterhill should lose its passenger service due to the expansion of tram services into the area. One of the reasons for the line being built was the competition between the Glasgow & South Western and the Caledonian who even built a line west of Potterhill which was never brought into use even though stations were built. The section of line north of Potterhill to Paisley lasted until 1917 before losing its passenger service.

Potterhill – Paisley West (Corsebar Junction)

Passenger service withdrawn	1 January 1917	*Station closed*		*Date*
Distance	1.5 miles	Potterhill		1 January 1917
Company	Glasgow & South Western			

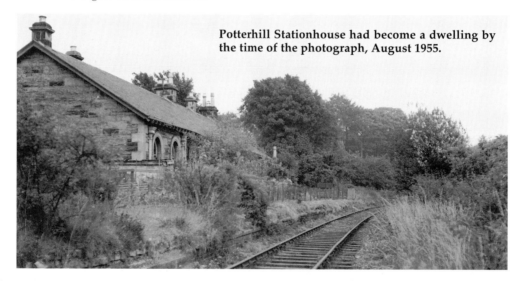

Potterhill Stationhouse had become a dwelling by the time of the photograph, August 1955.

Potterhill Station, opened in 1902, was about halfway between Paisley and Barrhead and formed part of the circular suburban service operated by the Glasgow & South Western. The circular service which linked Paisley with Glasgow via Barrhead or Crookston was cut back south of Potterhill in 1913 leaving only a service from Potterhill to Paisley and Glasgow. This only survived another four years before it too gave up the fight in the competition with trams and buses. Freight services lasted until 1959.

Renfrew Porterfield – Cardonald South (Cardonald South Junction)

Passenger service withdrawn	19 July 1926	*Stations closed*	*Date*
Distance	4.25 miles	Renfrew Porterfield	19 July 1926
Company	Glasgow & South Western/Caledonian	Kings Inch	19 July 1926
		Deanside	2 January 1905

During the expansion of railways into suburban areas at the end of the nineteenth century, areas like Renfrew had several lines built to provide local passenger services. Here and in the adjoining Paisley areas both the Caledonian and the Glasgow & South Western were in competition for both passenger and freight traffic. Renfrew was one of the last areas which did not have rail services so it was decided to link it and Erskine beyond to Cardonald on the Glasgow to Paisley line. However, due to opposition from the local landowner this scheme failed but what was constructed met some of the original proposals for the area. Built as the Glasgow & Renfrew District Railway, the line opened to passengers in June 1903 and the main Renfrew station was Kings Inch. After leaving there the line crossed the Paisley to Renfrew Wharf line, then made a U-turn to run parallel with this branch to Renfrew Porterfield Station which was adjacent to South Renfrew Station on the Renfrew Wharf line. Further plans were proposed which would have extended the line from Porterfield Station to Bishopton on the Gourock line from Paisley, but these never got off the ground. Deanside Station was built in a green field area which failed to develop and it closed after only three years in operation. Trains ran to and from Glasgow St Enoch and before closure there were about six return workings on weekdays. Once again, competition from trams was the reason for the line's closure but freight services lasted until 1964.

South Renfrew Station and the offices of Babcock & Wilcox, Renfrew.

Renfrew Wharf – Hillington West (Arkleston Junction)

		Stations closed	Date
Passenger service withdrawn	5 June 1967	Renfrew Wharf	5 June 1967
Distance	3.25 miles	South Renfrew	5 June 1967
Company	Glasgow & South Western	Sandyford	5 June 1967
		Abercorn	5 June 1967
		Paisley & Renfrew Station (Hamilton Street)	1 February 1866

A class 4 2-6-4T, no. 42247, at Sandyford Halt with the 6.05 p.m. from Renfrew Wharf to Glasgow St Enoch, July 1958.

Five stations served the Renfrew area and the branch line from Paisley to Renfrew Wharf was the first line to be built in the district. This served a large number of engineering works and the mainstay of passenger services over the years were workers' services coming from various parts of Glasgow. Sandyford Station was opened by the London, Midland & Scottish and throughout its life remained unadvertised in railway timetables as it was for use by workmen only. Like South Renfrew Station it had no freight facilities. Right up to the last, most services were steam operated and in the final days before closure it was only workers' services which used the line.

Uplawmoor – Neilston High

Passenger service withdrawn	2 April 1962	*Station closed*	*Date*
Distance	3 miles	Uplawmoor	2 April 1962
Company	Caledonian		

A diesel multiple unit at Uplawmoor Station, forming the 1.42 p.m. to Glasgow Central, 31 March 1962. This was the last departure before the closure of the station.

This three mile line formed part of what had been the Caledonian route from Glasgow to Ardrossan. Local passenger services between Uplawmoor to Ardrossan had been withdrawn in 1932 but the line remained in use as a through route for boat trains until 1947. When consideration was being given to electrifying the south side suburban routes in the early 1960s it was decided that they should only go as far as Neilston and the passenger service to Uplawmoor was subsequently withdrawn in April 1962. Freight services were withdrawn from Uplawmoor on the same date as the passenger service and the line was closed completely and lifted in December 1964.

Closed passenger stations on lines still open to passenger services

Line/Service   **Ardrossan Harbour – Ardrossan South Beach**

Station
Ardrossan Town

Date of closure
1 January 1968 (Reopened 19 January 1987)

Line/service   **Gourock – Paisley (Wallneuk Junction)**

Station
Bridge Street (Greenock)
Georgetown

Date of closure
1 June 1889
2 February 1959
(Known as Houston until 1 May 1926)

An English Electric Type 4 diesel, no. D296, at Cumnock Station with the midday Glasgow St Enoch to Carlisle service, September 1962.

Line/Service	**Gretna Junction – Glasgow via Dumfries**

Station	*Date of closure*
New Cumnock	6 December 1965 (reopened 27 May 1991)
Cumnock	6 December 1965
	(known as Old Cumnock until 10 January 1955)
Auchinleck	6 December 1965 (reopened 12 May 1984)
Mauchline	6 December 1965
Hurlford	7 March 1955
Kilmaurs	7 November 1966
	(reopened 12 May 1984 at a new location)

Station	*Date of closure*
Stewarton	7 November 1966 (reopened 5 June 1967)
Dunlop	7 November 1966 (reopened 5 June 1967)
Lugton	7 November 1966
Uplawmoor	7 November 1966
	(known as Caldwell until 2 April 1962)
Neilston Low	7 November 1966
	(known as Neilston until 24 January 1953)
Neilston (first)	1 May 1870

RAILWAY STATION, AUCHINLECK.

Engines lined up prior to scrapping at Hurlford Sheds, May 1961.

A Standard Class Five, no. 73124, passing through Neilston Low Station with a load of bananas from Greenock (James Watt Dock), August 1963.

Line/Service	**Largs – Kilwinning**	Station	Date of closure
		Dalrymple	6 December 1954
Station	*Date of closure*	Ayr (first)	1 July 1857
Saltcoats (first)	1 July 1858	Ayr Townhead or Southside	12 January 1886
Saltcoats (second)	1882	Monkton	28 October 1940
		Troon (first)	2 May 1892
Line/Service	**Stranraer Harbour – Glasgow ***	Gailes	2 January 1967
		Bogside	2 January 1967 (known as Bogside Race Course from 30 June 1952 to 14 June 1965)
Station	*Date of closure*	Dalry Junction	2 January 1860
Pinwherry	6 September 1965 (closed from 12 April 1886 to 14 June 1886)	Beith North	4 June 1951 (known as Beith until 2 June 1924)
Pinmore	6 September 1965 (closed from 12 April 1886 to 14 June 1886)	Howood	11 August 1840
		Howwood	7 March 1955
Killochan	1 January 1951	Miliken Park	18 April 1966 (reopened 16 May 1990)
Crosshill	1 March 1862	Elderslie	14 February 1966
Maybole (first)	24 may 1860		
Cassillis	6 December 1954		

PINMORE STATION.   RIDDEL PHOTO. GIRVAN.

*Before reaching Ayrshire this line passed through the stations of Castle Kennedy, Dunragit, New Luce and Glenwhilly. Details of these stations appear in *Dumfries & Galloway's Lost Railways*.

Pinwherry Ry Station & River Stinchar.

A Standard class 4 2-6-0, no. 76096, passes through Gailes Station with the 10.40 a.m. from Ayr to Glasgow St Enoch, August 1959.